# TWO CEREMONIES AT THE BORDER

*John murdered was at Carlinrigg*

# TWO CEREMONIES AT THE BORDER

## PETER ARMSTRONG

All rights reserved. No part of this work covered by the copyright herein may be reproduced or used in any means – graphic, electronic, or mechanical, including copying, recording, taping, or information storage and retrieval systems – without written permission of the publisher.

Printed by imprintdigital
Upton Pyne, Exeter
www.digital.imprint.co.uk

Typesetting and cover design by The Book Typesetters
hello@thebooktypesetters.com
07422 598 168
www.thebooktypesetters.com

Published by Shoestring Press
19 Devonshire Avenue, Beeston, Nottingham, NG9 1BS
(0115) 925 1827
www.shoestringpress.co.uk

First published 2023
© Copyright: Peter Armstrong
© Cover image: from *Border Ballads, Selected & Decorated with Woodcuts by Douglas Percy Bliss, Foreword by Herbert J.C. Grierson.* Courtesy of The Lit & Phil Library, Newcastle upon Tyne

The moral right of the author has been asserted.

ISBN 978-1-915553-38-6

# CONTENTS

A Requiem for Parcy Reed
    Preparation    3
    Introit    4
    Confetior    6
    Kyrie Eleison    7
    Word    8
    Creed    9
    Offertory    10
    Sanctus    11
    Consecration    12
    Communion    14
    Post Communion    16

The Fourteen Stations of Johnnie Armstrong
    Introit    21
    The First Station    22
    The Second Station    23
    The Third Station    24
    The Fourth Station    25
    The Fifth Station    26
    The Sixth Station    28
    The Seventh Station    29
    The Eighth Station    30
    The Ninth Station    31
    The Tenth Station    32
    The Eleventh Station    33
    The Twelfth Station    35
    The Thirteenth Station    36
    The Fourteenth Station    37
    Lament    38

Notes    40

# A Requiem for Parcy Reed

He knew that the tale he had to tell could not be one of final victory,
it could only be the record of what had had to be done,
and assuredly would have to be done again
in the never-ending fight against terror and its relentless onslaughts,
despite their personal afflictions, by all who,
while unable to be saints, but refusing to bow down
to pestilence, strive their utmost to be healers.

– Camus, *The Plague*

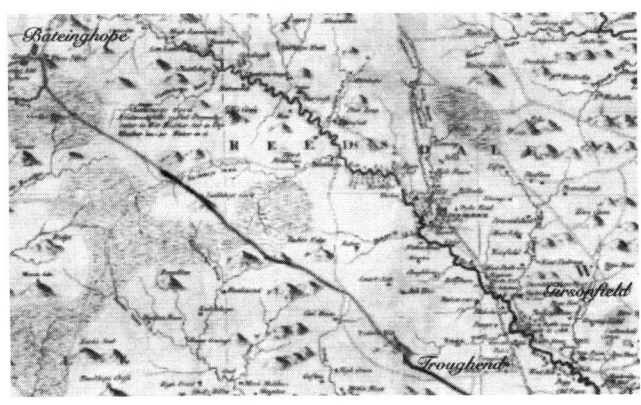

# PREPARATION

*Remember not, O Lord, our offences, nor those
of our fathers; neither take Thou vengeance on
our sins*

He's come and gone in the word of mouth,
he's off the record and away to the hope.
For vengeance or remission here's a song
to keep the blood fresh on the map.

Parcy's ghost's a flitting dove:
there's irony for a hunting man.
Tom, Will and John will leave
and Kitty chant for Telfer's pen

# INTROIT

> *Oh, Parcy Reed has ridden a raid*
> *Though he wad better hev stayed at hyem*
> *For the Fause-Hearted Haa's of Girsonfield*
> *It's them wi' him that he has taen*

*Judge me*

He pauses at the yard-gate
where a bell clatters in the wind
or a pail rings on the cobbles

and nods to himself or
some one or thing the rest
must guess

*Judge me*

Between one law and another
he goes to his altar
goes with or against
the grayne, the grey bowing grasses
of his little kingdom
his abattoir

Crows wheel away from the sycamore tops

Which god's ditched you, Parcy
or which devil?
And which if any
has distinguished
yours from any other's cause?

Law's the high ground
hope's the low
but one's as steep as the other
on the border side
and one by one
the gates beyond gates you've striven for
and are yours alone to enter
are shutting in front of you

# CONFETIOR

*O Parcy Reed has Crozier taen*
*And has delivered him tae the law,*
*But Crozier sez he will dee warse:*
*He'll gar the tower o Troughend faa*

Parcy puts his shoulder
to the stone of judgement

the steep law broods over
or mocks his labour

and come the summit look
how stone and keeper

hang by one another
against the pull of judgement

against blood against feud against kin
or god who plays this game with him

and still the kingdoms lie beneath
as if he'd power to choose between

—to cock a snook at death again?
or else bow down? And to whom bow down?

till down and down and down and down
come stone and trickster

stane-blind keeper
Reed unraed to Rede below

and that more bitter tease, the hope

# KYRIE ELEISON

*O Parcy Reed has Crozier taen*
*and has delivered him tae the law.*
*but Crozier says he will de warse*
*he'll gar the tower o' Troughen faa'*

It's all Greek on the borderside

to Parcy,
the stone of judgement weighed
in his righteous
maculate hand

to the slighted Halls
turning the bitter meat
of their belittlement
in the smoor
of a cold fire

to Crozier,
Parcy's cross shouldered
from Riccarton by Saughtree
and Wheelrig Head

to the altar
of their god
of the sleight of hand

# WORD

*For as a snare shall it*
*come upon you suddenly:*
*for as a snare shall it*
*come upon all that sit upon*
*the face of the whole earth*

*It's fower blades pierced him throw and throw*

Bog pool, hag, heugh
heather snare
and bracken snare
and sike in the tangle;
by Rooken Edge
the servant stumbles

Who'd believe
what we've heard?
Bruised reed trodden under
uncomely keeper
pierced
through
and through
and through whom
nothing.

Bruised Reed
trodden under
blemished ablation
broken.

# CREED

*Mr White, after remarking that there is no historical evidence to show when the events on which the ballad is founded occurred, informs us that almost every circumstance in the ballad has been transmitted to the present century by local tradition*

Whisper
at the half-door or the ingle

by Todhaugh
or Deadwater in the half-light

a hawk tracing
bruise-blue on the dusk-blue air

a form or form of words
to whisper or sing

in the code
of the valley's tongue

whereby no outsider
would hear or hearing grasp

the echo of its mutilated
mortal form.

How many ghosts of Parcy's ghost
have shape-shifted down the years

into this shape
we still believe

# OFFERTORY

*He's hunted up, he's hunted down*
*He's hunted aall the banks o' the Rede*
*Till weariedness has him owerta'en;*
*in the Baiteinghope he's laid his heid*

Here's Bateinghope, keeper
it's black burn fingering
the bait of the rock
the long
slow split
of the land

prefiguring.

Rest yourself. Rest
your exceeding weary
self. Let the wind across the heather
and the bent knuckles
of the hawthorn you lie under
sing you to thowless sleep
thouless oblation.

Tender Judases attend you
and, for your angel
a buzzard above Cross Cleugh.

Poor buzzard-bait Parcy
you have offered yourself up
and the sacrifice

is acceptable

# SANCTUS

*He had but time to cross himsel*
*A prayer he hadna time to say*
*Till round him came the Croziers keen*
*All riding graithed and in array*

In the moment he turns
from his shamefaced
outfaced betrayers

and outstares the gloat
and slaver of his killers
he sees

in the shiver of the heather
in the fells'
infinite slow flow

all his thrones and angels;
between the curlew and the lark
and the wind's clamour

all his praises and hosannas
cry. Death a coal to his lips
what lucid prophecies

had he time
might crown
his going down

# CONSECRATION

> *They've set upon him all at ance;*
> *they've mangled him maste cruellie;*
> *the slightest wound had caused his deid*
> *and they hae gien him thirty-three*

He crosses himself and receives
thirty three wounds:
one for each of Christ's life's

years; which make no amends
which settle, for all their taunts,
no debt. Past grounds

for hope or fear, for once
and maybe all he sees
fate and chance

as equal follies
of law and feud,
blood-fellows

he has lived
and now is dying by.
The kin and chattels loved

and found good currency
in the potter's field's
blood-black, black blood economy

he now yields
as he does breath.
Kine to their folds,

blood to the heath,
night falls
on mere individual death;

out on the fell
some circling beast outlives
each and all

and a famished wind grieves

# COMMUNION

> *so far did they carry out their sanguinary measures even against his lifeless body, that tradition says the fragments thereof had to be collected together and conveyed in pillow slips home to Troughend*
>
> Richardson's Table Book p 362
>
> *They've hackèd off his hands and feet*
> *And left him lying in the lea*

Sanguis Domini nostri custódiat

Keep, Keeper, kept;
cupped mebbies
in the cross-carriers'

tender bloody hands
before or after
ablation

after ablation. Surely
a thousand Croziers
in each matted slaughterman

to warrant such
distribution of the gift,
such scraps to glean

from the giving.
How close, the five of them;
how piously they celebrate;

how deep their preservation
and the blood-bond between
the living and the dead

and the soon-to-be-dead
and the soon-to-be-killers
for ever and ever

amen

# POST COMMUNION

*It was the hour of gloaming gret*
*When hords come yhem to fold and pen*
*A herdsman spied a hunter lie;*
*sez he 'can this be the laird Troughend?*

Five ride west, three east
and leave the mutilated man
still breathing on the bent.

Judgement, blame and consequence
bleed away
with all his properties.

(see from his ankles and his wrists);
and if he bows, is it pestilence
or plain weariedness

has felled him?
To be one and one alone
and all his altars fallen.

Moss for ablution, cotton grass and bracken
and blood-dark peat
to sop the lees

of his element;
but no great wind, no quake
no fire; and no voice

unless our voices
less to ask his being there
than bear witness

to his unsaintly ending,
the healing striven for
and the affliction found.

# The Fourteen Stations of Johnnie Armstrong

'Nowadays people must not trust each other before
the very last binding seal is affixed.
And even that is not enough'

– Montaigne

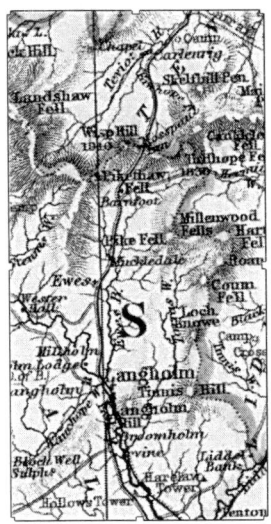

# INTROIT

*Had I my horse and my harness gude*
*and ryding as I wont to be*
*It sould haif bene tald these hundred yeir*
*The meiting of my king and me*

Close on five, John
and still told, tald, telt.
Dryden, Pepys and Ritson,
Scott and Herd and tuneless Child
all move their caps
or rake your ashes.

A few still sing,
still trace their one warm
debatable line
by Liddel and Esk,
by blood,

as if there were
some passage back

some trick
to raise these bones

to light, breath, air

# THE FIRST STATION

*The King he writes him a lovin' letter*
*in his ain hand se tenderly...*

He loves this.

From his high window
he looks down

on the mists and tempests of his state;

far-sighted in his clear air,
with the serenity of power
almost his to grasp

looks on the Borders,
that dark error
that slippery country.

It is not his enough

He holds it in his gaze,
and on the page
and the pity of things

writes
in a loveless hand

and feels rising in himself
the love of the act

# THE SECOND STATION

> *...An he's sent it te Johnnie Airmstrang*
> *Come speak wi me maist speedily*

He errs this once

and flattery has the better of his guile:
*In his own hand!*
        or *the one I shall kiss.*

Was he a reading man? He listens, then.
Watch him in the fire-flicker;
another cup, perhaps,
no bloodsweat – this is his night

# THE THIRD STATION

*They ran their horse on Langum Howm*
*And brake their speirs with meckle main;*
*The ladies lukit frae their loft-windows*
*'God bring our men well back again!'*

The women know
as all those Spanish Madonnas know
far better than the infant king,

than John, that violent Christ
who rides
more crowned than graithed

to lying Jamie,
his spineless Pilate

# THE FOURTH STATION

> *'May I find grace, my lord and liege,*
> *grace for my loyal men and me?*
> *My name it is Johnnie Armstrang*
> *and subject te yersel' says he*

He falls a second time.
His footing that was cocksure
slithers
      and the rest must follow; thus
he hands himself
into his hangman's hands.

Gangmeister Jamie lords it;
King Johnnie
rues his genuflexion

But pokerfaced, borderfaced, feudfaced,
will outface his boy king

and who wouldn't mop that face for an icon?
and who wouldn't sing
his via dolorosa

# THE FIFTH STATION

*Grant me my lyfe, my liege, my king,*
*And a bony gift I'll gie te thee;*
*Full fower-and-tweny milk-whyt steids*
*were a' foald in a yeir te me*

*…Gude fower-and -twenty gangin' mills*

*…Bauld fower-and-twent sisters sons*

He haggles.
He knows this game's
rites and subtleties,
the antiphonal pulse
of barter,
blackmail,
bloodmoney.

A tilt of the head, a nod,
a pursing of the lips;
words but necessary
cloth to clothe
the ritual.

But Jamie winnit play, fa-la
so Johnnie cannit win

Foals for the fond feul, then;
gold for his eyelids;
mills for the grinding of him;
grain for the grayne's grief;
sisters' sons
to bear his bier.

Here's dice, Johnnie;
roll them for your cloak,
your kine, your kin,
your blood, your good name:
the indivisible fabric
of the nothing that's left you

# THE SIXTH STATION

*Away, away thou traytor strang!*
  *Out of my sicht thou mayst sune be!*
  *I grantit nivvor a traytor's lyfe*
  *And now I'll not begin with thee*

Traitor, then,
he hands himself over

and enters his passion.

He laughs
and his poor sleepwalkers

rouse themselves a moment
and laugh

as children
laugh unknowingly.

Christjohnnie's true to the end;
called to his Gethsemane

he needs must come;
Judasjohnnie's jumped the gun

to hasten in the kingdom

# THE SEVENTH STATION

*Away, away thou traytor strang!*
*Out of my sicht thou mayst sune be!*
*I grantit nivvor a traytor's lyfe*
*And now I'll not begin with thee*

Here's Jamie's refrain again:

strang, strong, strung
along and soon up.

Is it from fear
or common speech,

that lost syllable?
Strang? You have said it.

But here, but now:
a mockery? Hail, king of

and even here, and even now
should Johnnie say or could he

his three thousand angels
would fly down or

the people choose
him – but

Christjohnnie or Johnniebarabbas
one or other hangs

# THE EIGHTH STATION

*Ye lied, ye lied, now king, he said*
*althocht a king and prince ye be*
*for I luid naithing in all my life*
*I dare well say it, but honesty*

Game over, John,
and you with it

and the truth of the lie
comes clear

and James, lightfingered with the law,
lays it down;

brave before God,
has no answer for the man;

and John sits
in judgement on his judge.

Or the truth
dawns on him,

truth-lover, or ironist
at the last

or, the pair of them,
philosophers, like Pilate

who can see how clean
their equally bloody hands

truly are

# THE NINTH STATION

*To seik het water beneath cauld yce,*
*It surely is a great folie;*
*and aah've socht grace of a graceless face*
*wheor it was nivver wont te be*

Beneath that ice, John
beneath the grace
of his high palaces
beneath this graceless
sleight-of-hand,
this face-off,
this loss of face
for one of you or both;

beneath that cold skin,
as under Esk waters wintering
and Teviot locked in,
water is a cold smoke churning
and angry for the spring.

Look at him again:
this is his spring.
And you? a haugh of a man,
thaw water will bear away
in its unkind baptism

# THE TENTH STATION

*There hang nine targats at Johnnie's hat*
*and Ilk an worth three hundred pound:*
*'What wants that knave that a king suld haif,*
*But the sword of honour and the crown?'*

Silver's not rich enough
for the border king,

who makes himself
a gilt offering;

whose cap of gold's
a crown of thorns;

whose belt's
a noose of gold.

Now James can buy
his potter's field, the Borders;

his field of blood,
his debatable bargain.

Come back here a man, boy-king,
to bury yourself.

# THE ELEVENTH STATION

> 'O whair gat thou those targats, Johnnie,
>   That blink sae brawly abune thy brie?'
> 'I gat them in the field fechting,
>   Where, cruel king, thou durst not be.'

He sits there agleam
in his wry self,

little king, yauld grew,
cornered tod;

now all the patter
of blood barter's done with,

rises
into his full self

to taunt;
gaunt in his saddle,
to prophecy:

*here's sick James abed
while his petty army
dithers on the moss;*

*here the winner
of John's seamless lands*

*turns his back on the field
and a king's face to the wall:*

No Flowers of the Forest
for the Gudeman of Ballengiech:

History drips
from the victor's pen

onto the winner's page
but song owes it nothing

# THE TWELFTH STATION

> 'And God be withee, Kirsty, my son,
> Whair thou sits on they nurse's knee!
> But and thou live this hundred yeir
> Thy fathers better thoult never be'

No *Mother,*
*Behold your son* then;
no *Madonna con bambino*
in John's
mind's
eye.

Here's Kirsty
on his nurse's knee,
a weak branch
of a cursed tree

and the house more prized,
more praised
these last few minutes
as John sees

his little kingdom,
his bloody kirk
prised free
of his tied hands

# THE THIRTEENTH STATION

*John murdered was at Carlinrigg*
*And all his gallant companie;*
*But Scotland's heart was never sae wae*
*To see sae mony brave men die.*

So: Carlin-rigg.

Are we two Sundays back
from your passion, John?

Or on hags' ground?

Or remembering your silver
if not your gold?

Or are these thistles, John,
hungry, bitter plants,
drawing out your sap
where you lie
shall we say
sleeping?

Or just heather
persisting on its acid soil,
blood red for you in summer, John,
or porphyry for James
and his brief, bloody rule?

# THE FOURTEENTH STATION

No Joseph's tomb for Johnnie
and for this last station
no last verse.

We know the picture, though:
the knot of bodies
in a roadside ditch,

their dispatchers
blankly at their ease.
They smoke. They look away.

Did they throw dice
for your cloak, Johnnie?
Did they itemise your gold?

Did they strip you
of your self
before they put you down?

Welcome to Gehenna, then:
three days reiving here
and you might rise

if this is rising
in the dark gospel
of a ballad

# LAMENT

So, Solmon-Sanhedrin-James; O fountainhead;
what waers have you fouled today?
What vlley deepened? What fell raised?

Carlinrigg's no even ground:
John's come up by Braeheid
and down by Linhope,

by the lank bent
and the brent pasture
and his flower's gone in a day.

Flow sickly, Teviot;
run dry, Esk and Liddel;
drain bare, Solway:

the commonweal's awry.

*Crosier Says he will dee warse*
*He'll gar the tower o' troughend faa*

# NOTES

*A Requiem for Parcy Reed*

These poems each take as their stepping-off point a verse or part of a verse of the ballad *The Death of Parcy Reed* (Roud Folksong Index 335; Child's English & Scottish Popular Ballads 193). The sequence also follows the structure of the Mass. The quotations in the text & in these notes are taken from The Daily Missal and Liturgical Manual of 1955, revised by Rev J Dukes SJ, published by Laverty & Sons, Leeds. (Henceforth referred to as 'Daily Missal'). The copy I have been using was my father's.

Parcy Reed, of Troughend (pronounced 'Trowend') on the Western flank of Redesdale was the 'Keeper' of that part of the English Middle March, abutting the Scottish border. A Keeper was responsible for maintenance (if the term is realistically applicable) of law within a particular area of the March – Tynedale and Redesdale in England, Liddesdale in Scotland. In this capacity he arrested one of the Crozier (or Crosier or Croser) family, whose stronghold stood across the border at Riccarton in Liddesdale. By way of revenge, the Croziers enlisted the assistance of the Hall family of Girsonfield, close by Otterburn and about a mile distant from Parcy's home. Parcy, with ill judgement, went hunting with the Halls, ending the trip exhausted in the high valley of Bateinghope, close by the border and much closer to the Croziers' stronghold than to his own home. While he slept, the Halls disarmed him and stood by as the Croziers approached to this prearranged rendezvous and proceeded to slaughter Reed.

*Preparation*

*Remember not...* Daily Missal 'Preparation for Holy Mass' p 889

*hope – a valley*

*flitting dove* – there are different tales of Parcy's ghost with respect to the form it took – a dove, a hawk or other flying creature – and the precise (or imprecise) area of Redesdale that it haunted

*Tom, Will and John* – the Hall brothers who betrayed Parcy. Even for those wild days, their actions were so derided that they were driven from Redesdale

*Kity... Telfer* See Child *English and Scottish Popular Ballads Vol IV 1890 (Loomis House 2007) pp 35, 37.* A version of the ballad was collected by James Telfer from the singing of Catherine or Kitty Hall

*Introit*

*Judge me* – Daily Missal 'Preparatory prayers at the foot of the altar' – Psalm 42 Catholic bible, 43 others

*grayne* – Family, clan

*Law's the high ground* – 'law' is a common suffix for hill names in the far north of England and southern Scotland

*gates beyond gates* – *see* Kafka, *The Trial* C9

*Confetior*

> *Parcy puts his shoulder* – see Camus, *The Myth of Sysyphus*
>
> *and still the kingdoms* – Matthew C4, V8
>
> *To cock a snook* – Camus again, citing the legend that Sysyphus incurred the gods' wrath by tricking his way out of the underworld back into the land of the living.
>
> *unraed* – unwise
>
> *hope* 'The upland part of a mountain valley. The inch ordnance map of Northumberland give seventy-three place-names having this termination. In the County of Durham forty such occur' *Northumberland Words. A Glossary of words used in Northumberland and on Tyneside.* Richard Oliver Heslop. English Dialect Society/OUP 1893-4

*Kyrie Eleison*

> *Title 'Kyrie Eleison' ('Lord have Mercy')* is the only part of the Latin Mass to retain the Greek
>
> *stone of judgement* – John C8, V7. 'He that is without sin among you, let him first cast a stone…'
>
> *slighted Halls.* Some sources hold that the Halls were passed over in favour of Parcy Reed for the keepership of Redesdale, hence their treachery
>
> *Riccarton.* Riccarton Tower, in Liddesdale, just over the border from the headwaters of the North Tyne, was the stronghold of the Croziers.

*Saughtree* (pr 'sofftree') *Wheelrig Head*. Possible route the Croziers would have followed from Riccarton to the Bateinghope if they were following old roads, although following roads would not be guaranteed on the part of raiding parties crossing the border.

## Word

> *heugh* (pr. 'hyooff' or 'hyuff') – 'a precipitous hill, a cliff or dell with steep sides, but without a stream in it' Heslop ibid.
>
> *Bruised reed*. Isaiah C42, V3 'A bruised reed he will not break'
>
> *uncomely keeper* Isaiah C53, V1. Both verses and other passages of Isaiah's *Servant Songs* were taken up by New Testament writers as prophetic of Jesus' sufferings.
>
> *ablation*. 'Removal of any part of the body' Concise OED

## Creed

> *Mr White etc*. See above citation of *Child* in Preparation
>
> *Todhaugh*. Pr. 'half' or 'hoff' 'an alluvial flat or stretch of low-lying land on a riverside' Heslop ibid. Typically bound on three sides by a meander of the river.
>
> *a hawk*. See note to 'flitting dove' in Preparation above

*Offertory*

*Bateinghope.* Bateinghope Burn is the furthest upstream significant tributary on the south side of the River Rede. Its valley was the scene of Parcy's murder

*bait. 'the grain or cleavage of wood or stone'* Chambers Scots Dictionary

*thowless.* 'wanting in energy, useless' Heslop, ibid

**Sanctus**

*In the moment he turns.* 'Sisyphus, proletarian of the gods, powerless and rebellious, knows the whole extent of his wretched condition: it is what he thinks of during is descent. The lucidity that was to constitute his torture at the same time crowns his victory' Camus *The Myth of Sisyphus* trans J O'Brien Penguin 1979 p109

*thrones and angels, a coal to his lips.* Isaiah C6, vs1-6 '*Then flew on of the seraphim to me having in his hand a burning coal which he had taken from the altar. And he touched my mouth, and said: 'Behold, this has touched your lips; your guilt is taken away and your sin forgiven.'* RSV

*Lucid Prophecies.* Hamlet Act V, Sc II 341 & 360

*going down.* Psalm 115, V17:

*The dead do not praise the Lord,*
  *nor do any that go down into silence*
RSV

*Consecration*

*famished* Growing up, I was familiar with this being used to mean 'very cold' as well as hungry. Collins dictionary identifies this as an Irish usage.

*Communion*

*Sanguis Domini nostri custódiat*

More fully 'Sanguis Domini nostri Jesu Christi ánimam tuam in vitam æternam'

The Priest takes the Chalice and making the sign of the Cross with it says: The blood of our Lord Jesus Christ preserve my soul unto life everlasting' Daily Missal p 962-3

*Surely a thousand* 5 X 1000 gives you 5000 to feed.

*Post Communion*

*Five ride west, three east.* The five Croziers back over the border to Liddesdale, the three Hall brothers towards their home at Girsonfield, above Otterburn in Redesdale

*all his altars fallen… wind, voice etc.* See 1 Kings C 19

## The Fourteen Stations of Johnnie Armstrong

Each poem takes as its start-point a verse from the ballad of Johnnie Armstrong (Roud Folksong Index 76; Child's English & Scottish Popular Ballads 169). Johnny Armstrong was, perhaps the border reiver par excellence: a wily operator in a lawless society and landscape, making the best of those circumstances for himself and his extended family; or a plain lawless thug and extortionist, a mafioso before the Mafia – depending on your point of view. He was the most important operator in the Debatable Lands, a section of the western border marches between England and Scotland that answered in no strict way to the rule of either kingdom. It was said that his power was so extensive that the Armstrongs could put three thousand men on horseback if needed. Unsurprisingly, such a powerful individual with what might be thought of as his own private army was seen as a threat by the young James V of Scotland, who was in the business of asserting royal power without much care for the rule of law. in 1530 James offered to meet Johnny, giving him safe passage to a meeting place near the headwaters of the River Teviot, crucially just outside of Johnny's safe haven of the Debatable Lands. There Johnny & his men were summarily arrested and hanged. (James was greatly invested in strengthening the rule of the crown, but not much interested in the rule of law).

The Stations of the Cross are a devotion in the Catholic, Anglican and Lutheran Christian traditions, marking the steps from Jesus' 'trial' under Pontius Pilate to his death on the cross and burial

*Introit*

*Warm line/passage back* – See Stan Rogers' song *North West Passage*.

*Dryden, Pepys etc* – ballad collectors.

*tuneless Child* – Probably the best-known ballad collector today, Francis James Child, 1825-1896, was collector/author of The English and Scottish Popular Ballads, now simply known as 'Child.' Strangely, he had no interest whatever in the ballads as songs. All of the verses quoted in the 'Stations' are taken from the Loomis House Press, 2nd edition Vol 3.

## The First Station

*From his high window etc* – "no pleasure is comparable to the standing on the vantage ground of truth (a hill not to be commanded, and where the air is always clear and serene) and to see the errors and wanderings, and mists and tempests, in the vale below; so always that this prospect be with pity and not with swelling or pride."

(Francis Bacon – Of Truth, including Bacon's paraphrasing of Lucretius' De Rerum Natura)

See also The Pity, Ken Smith, in the collection of that name, Jonathan Cape 1967 & The Poet Reclining, Bloodaxe Books 1982.

## The Third Station

*Spanish Madonnas* – for instance see the collection in Pamplona cathedral museum, particularly of romanesque polychrome figures of the Madonna and Child.

*Graithed* – equipped, armed, apparelled.

## The Fourth Station

*hands himself* – see The Stature of Waiting, WH Vanstone, Darton, Longman and Todd, London 1982, a meditation on the betrayal of Jesus by Judas. Vanstone bases his reflections on the absence of "betrayal" in the vocabulary of the Gospel writers' description of the act of Judas, which is more accurately translated, he argues, as "handing over" & marks the transition, he maintains, from the activity of Jesus to his passive receipt of suffering.

*Gangmeister/King* – "Remove justice and what are kingdoms but gangs of criminals on a large scale. What are criminal gangs but petty kingdoms?"

Augustine, City of God Book IV C4

Where the king is unjust…or the nobles are unjust…or the people are unjust then… the commonwealth is not corrupted…it ceases to exist at all.

Book 1I Chapter 21

*mop that face for an icon.* There is a tradition that St Veronica mopped Christ's face on his way to Calvary, gaining an imprint of it, said to have miraculous powers. Her name translates as "True Icon" & there is no evidence of her existence.

## The Fifth Station

*grayne* – Family, clan. 'a branch or fork in a river or a tree… also the branch or tine of a fork… grain, or grayne passes to mean the branches of the ancient and powerful families that inhabited Tynedale and the branching valleys of the district'

Northumberland Words, Vol 2 G-Z. English Dialect Society/ OUP 1893-4

*Dice/indivisible fabric* – John 19. 23-25 'When the soldiers had crucified Jesus, they took his garments and made four parts, one for each soldier; also his tunic. But the tunic was without seam, woven from top to bottom; so they said to one another 'let us not tear it, but cast lots for it to see whose it shall be..' All biblical quotes from the Revised Standard Version

## The Sixth Station

*He laughs* – See The Gospel of Judas, Ed. Kasser, Meyer & Wurst, National Geographic 2006, a translation from the Coptic of the Codex Tchacos, a ?2nd century gnostic gospel that both reframes Judas as standing out from the other apostles in grasping the true nature of Jesus, and introducing the motif "Jesus laughed" on several occasions – usually at his followers' lack of understanding.

*his poor sleepwalkers* -Matthew 24 vss 40-46 'And he came to them and found them sleeping…'

## The Seventh Station

*You have said it* – Matthew 27 v11 'Now Jesus stood before the governor; and the governor asked him, 'Are you the King of the Jews?' Jesus said, 'You have said so.'

*Hail king of*- Matthew 27 28-31 'And kneeling before him they mocked him, saying, 'Hail, King of the Jews!'

*three thousand angels* – Matthew 26 53. See also GM Frazer's The Steel Bonnets, Harper Collins 1971, 1994; p57 "In Johnnie Armstrong's day (c.1528) they [i.e. the Armstrongs and the Elliots] could put 3000 men into the saddle, and probably did more damage by foray than any other two families combined."

*Christjohnnie or Johnniebarabbas* – Matthew 27 15-23 'Do you think I could not appeal to my Father, and he will at once send me more than twelve legions of angels?'

## The Eighth Station

John 18.37 "Jesus said "You say that I am king.. For this I was born and for this I have come into the world, to bear witness to the truth. Everyone who is in the truth hears my voice." Pilate said to him "What is the truth?"

*philosophers* – see Francis Bacon On Truth: "'What is truth?' said jesting Pilate, and would not stay for an answer… But it is not only the difficulty and labour which men take in finding out of truth; nor again, that, when it is found, it imposeth upon men's thoughts; that doth bring lies in favour; but a natural, though corrupt love of the lie itself."

## The Ninth Station

*haugh* – a river meadow, the low-lying land partially enclosed by a river's meander.

*Esk/Teviot* John had ridden from the Esk valley, that drains south into the Solway, over the watershed into the valley of the Teviot, a tributary of the Tweed. In doing so he left the Debatable land, his stronghold.

## The Tenth Station

*his potter's field* – Matthew 27. 3-8 The field bought as a burial ground with the thirty pieces of silver returned by the repentant, despairing Judas.

*his field of blood* – the name given to the field.

*Come back here a man, boy-king,* – James was only 17 when he had John put to death.

*bury yourself* – See here's *sick James abed,* below.

## The Eleventh Station

*yauld grew* – old greyhound. See James Armstrong's Kielder Hunt in Wanny Blossoms, Hexham 1879, digitally available at:

https://archive.org/details/wannyblossomsboo00armsrich

*tod* – a fox.

*here's sick James abed etc* – James's final illness appears to have set in at or following the battle of Solway Moss, 1542, in which he did not participate and which ended in humiliating defeat for his army.

*winner of John's seamless lands* – After John's execution, James granted his lands to Robert, Lord Maxwell, Scottish Warden of the West March. Apparently humiliated by James's choice of a commoner to lead the army, he withdrew from the field at Solway Moss.

*Flowers of the Forest* – commemorates the death of James's father James IV at the battle of Flodden Field, 1513.

*Gudeman of Ballengiech* There were various comic tales told and songs sung of James going about in disguise under this name, either to spy incognito on his subjects, or to meet with his various mistresses.

## The Twelfth Station

*Mother, Behold your son* – John 19.27 'When Jesus saw his mother, and the disciple whom he loved standing there, , he said to his mother, 'Woman, behold, your son!'

## The Thirteenth Station

A piece of fanciful etymology. Perhaps carlin=heather (see below) is the likeliest derivation, but perhaps not, assuming it was one heather-topped ridge among many…

*two Sundays back* – From the rhyme to remember the Sundays of lent and Easter: Tid, Mid, Miseray; Carlin, Palm & Paste-egg day.

*hag* – 'Carlin, Carline… an old woman; a shrew, hag…' Chambers Scots Dictionary

*silver* – 'carline… a small silver coin…' Shorter OED

*thistles* – '…In *full carline thistle*. A spiny plant of the genus Carlina' Shorter OED

*heather* – 'Carlin' heather… fine-leaved heath, bell-heather' Chambers Scots Dictionary

*The Fourteenth Station*

*No Joseph's tomb* – John 19. 38-42 Joseph of Arimathea 'who was a disciple of Jesus, but secretly… asked Pilate that he might take away the body of Jesus, and Pilate gave him leave.' RSV

*Did they throw dice* – See note to 5th Station.

*Gehenna* – Generally a synonym for 'Hell' since New Testament times. Originally Ge-Hinnom, a valley near Jerusalem associated with child sacrifices and subsequently a rubbish-dump.

*Lament*

*fountainhead etc* – See Francis Bacon On Judicature, quoting Proverbs 25.26 and Isaiah 40 'Above all things, integrity is their [i.e. judges'] portion and proper virtue. 'Cursed' (saith the law) 'is he that removeth the landmark.' …But it is the unjust judge that is the capital remover of landmarks, when he defineth amiss of land and property. One foul sentence doth more hurt than many foul examples; for these do but corrupt the stream, the other corrupteth the fountain–so saith Solomon: 'The just man failing in his cause before his adversary is like a troubled fountain and a corrupted vein."

*Bent* – '…as the ballad writers called the rough white-grass moor.' GM Trevelyan The Middle Marches, 1934, 1976

*Brent* – burned; also steep, Chambers Scots Dictionary

*Image Sources*

Front Cover and Frontispiece – from *Border Ballads, Selected & Decorated with Woodcuts by Douglas Percy Bliss, Foreword by Herbert J.C. Grierson*. Courtesy of The Lit & Phil Library, Newcastle upon Tyne

Parcy Reed Title Page Map – from *The Middle Marches*, Robert Bertram, in *The Middle Marches,* GM Trevelyan, 1934, 1976, Northumberland and Newcastle Society/Frank Graham

Johnnie Armstrong Title Page Map – from *New travelling map of Scotland*. Alexander Keith Johnston, engraved by W & AK Johnston 1858. Courtesy of the National Library of Scotland map archive https://maps.nls.uk/

Endpiece – Bliss, ibid.